Gary and Maths

Written by William Mather and Bridget Mather-Scott

Illustrated by William Mather and Amélie Kerslake

Gary and Maths
Published by Billy Bees Learning in 2023
International House, 64 Nile Street, London, N1 7SR
billybeeslearning.co.uk

"Everyone finds maths tricky at some point"

Professor Steve Chinn

Welcome to our book, it's great to have you here!

Before we start, let's have a look at what dyslexia and dyscalculia are...

Dyslexia

"dis-lex-ee-ah"

Dyslexia is a learning difficulty. As well as affecting reading and writing it causes difficulties with remembering things, organisation, and processing information.

Working memory holds information temporarily and 'works out' problems and answers; like using a scrap piece of paper for writing rough notes or workings out. Dyslexic people have a smaller working memory...it's like having a sticky note to do rough work on, instead of a whole page.

Dyscalculia

"dis-kal-k yoo-lee-ah"

Dyscalculia is a maths learning difficulty affecting the ability to acquire mathematical skills and understand numbers.

It affects people differently, both at school and home. Basic sums and complex sums can be tricky, as well as making estimations and understanding quantities, weights, speeds and distances.

Gary and Maths

This is Gary.

Gary has dyscalculia, which can make learning tricky.

Dyscalculia also means Gary has trouble remembering things, which is a bit of a pain...

Actually it's a massive pain.

Gary's best friends are Joe and Toby.

They all go to Middlewood High School.

This is mini Gary. He lives happily in Gary's brain,

and helps Gary with his learning!

Here are Gary's teachers...

ART
Mr Squiggle

MATHS
Mr Bramley

SCIENCE
Mr Conical

MUSIC
Mr Trumpet

P.E
Mr Wilson

ENGLISH
Mrs Flump

Today Gary has maths with Mr Bramley.

Mr Bramley can be quite grumpy and smells slightly of oranges.

Maths can make Gary worry.

And this stops Gary (and mini Gary) from thinking clearly.

Gary has learnt that taking deep breaths can helps him to feel calmer

..and off goes mini Gary to
work out the answer...

Well, whenever he gets interrupted, mini Gary has to start all over again.

Oh and whenever a question is timed, or Gary is told to "hurry up" these guys appear and make it harder.

Too many "hurry up's" and time pressures mean mini Gary can't get past all the chaos and fire dudes

After a few attempts mini Gary gets too tired to try again.

The trouble is, Mr Bramley doesn't really care how many coins mini Gary gets.

Mr Bramley just cares about getting as many right answers as possible, as quickly as possible.

Gary didn't expect Mr Bramley to ask that question...
maybe his oranges had been extra tasty today.

Tasty or not, Gary felt happy.

That evening, Gary put together some information to share with Mr Bramley.

This is what he found...

Dyscalculics/dyslexics often have to self regulate to calm panic and anxiety

...this takes up time and energy. It can happen several times a day and is EXHAUSTING.

Dyscalculics / dyslexics are great problem solvers!
They often have to find different ways of doing things -
like how mini Gary split 3x12 into three simpler sums.

This takes a lot of resilience and not giving up!
It's hard work and takes much longer.

We hope you found our book interesting!

Written by Bridget and Will to raise
awareness of dyscalculia and dyslexia.

BVPRI - #0006 - 081123 - C46 - 215/215/3 - PB - 9601141000020 - Gloss Lamination